THE WORLD AROUND US

ON OUR STREET

Our First Talk About Poverty

Dr. Jillian Roberts and Jaime Casap   Illustrations by Jane Heinrichs

ORCA BOOK PUBLISHERS

*To my husband, Stephen, who has helped me become the best version of myself
and who has empowered me to try to make a difference in the world. — JR*

*To my children, Elaine, William and Azella,
who I know will change the world for the better! — JC*

For my daughter, Mary. — JH

Library and Archives Canada Cataloguing in Publication

Roberts, Jillian, 1971–, author
On our street: our first talk about poverty / Dr. Jillian Roberts, Jaime Casap;
illustrated by Jane Heinrichs.
(The world around us)

Includes bibliographical references.
Issued in print and electronic formats.
ISBN 978-1-4598-1617-6 (hardcover).—ISBN 978-1-4598-1618-3 (pdf).—
ISBN 978-1-4598-1619-0 (epub)

1. Poverty—Juvenile literature. 2. Homelessness—Juvenile literature. I. Heinrichs,
Jane, 1982–, illustrator II. Casap, Jaime, 1967–, author III. Title.
HC79.P6R63 2018   j362.5   C2017-904515-6
C2017-904516-4

Summary: Using illustrations, full-color photographs and
straightforward text, this nonfiction picture book introduces
the topics of homelessness and poverty to young readers.

First published in the United States, 2018
Library of Congress Control Number: 2017949691

*Orca Book Publishers is dedicated to preserving the environment and has
printed this book on Forest Stewardship Council® certified paper.*

Orca Book Publishers gratefully acknowledges the support for
its publishing programs provided by the following agencies:
the Government of Canada through the Canada Book Fund and
the Canada Council for the Arts, and the Province of British Columbia
through the BC Arts Council and the Book Publishing Tax Credit.

Artwork created using English watercolors and
Japanese brush pens on Italian watercolor paper.

Cover and interior art by Jane Heinrichs
Edited by Liz Kemp
Design by Rachel Page

Front cover photos by iStock.com: © asiseeit, mihailomilovanovic, SinanAyhan
Interior photo credits: by iStock.com: © pinoteross p. 4, Zinkevych p. 5, kaetana p. 5,
SlobodanMiljevic p. 7, xavierarnau p. 8, SinanAyhan p 10, xavierarnau p. 11,
finwal p. 12, max-kegfire p. 13, asiseeit p. 14, kMickey p 15, Nomadsoul1 p. 16,
dabldy p. 17, bodnarchuk p. 18, Imgorthand p. 19, didesign021 p. 19,
FatCamera p. 20, pixelfusion3d p. 21, shironosov p. 22, jcarillet p. 24,
sadikgulec p. 25, verve231 p. 25, andykazie p. 26, Stacey Newman p. 27, asiseeit p. 28;
Stocksy United: © Cameron Whitman p. 5, Rob and Julia Campbell p. 9;
Shutterstock.com © pisaphotography p. 6

ORCA BOOK PUBLISHERS
www.orcabook.com

Printed and bound in Canada.

21 20 19 18 • 5 4 3 2

○—○

When you venture out into the world around us, you may notice things that are new to you. The world is filled with unique people, who live in a variety of different ways. Sometimes people are happy in these different situations, and sometimes they are not. It's okay to ask questions when you do not understand the way another person is living.

○—○—○—○—○—○—○—   —○—○—○—○—○—○—○

On the walk to school today, I saw
a man sleeping on the street.
He had all his belongings around him.
Why would he sleep outside?

That person is sleeping on the street because he does not have a permanent place to live. That person is *homeless*. People who are homeless live on the street, or they live in community shelters. Sometimes they move between shelters, or between shelters and the street. People who are homeless are often in that situation because of *poverty*. Poverty is a big problem in our world today.

What Is Homelessness?

When people live on the streets or without a permanent shelter or living quarters, we say they are homeless. This includes people who live in or move between community shelters.

What Is Poverty?

Poverty can mean a lot of different things. The simplest definition is that a person doesn't have enough money for food, clothing and shelter. But poverty can also mean not having a good job or being unable to go to school or to the doctor. It can mean feeling unsafe or excluded or like you don't have opportunities in life to be happy.

What is it like to live on the streets?

It's hard to live on the streets. People there are exposed to all kinds of weather, and they can become sick when they can't keep dry and warm. People who are homeless are often hungry. Even if they have enough money to buy food, they don't have a place to cook meals. They may feel lonely or judged by others, and they may be treated poorly or be the victims of violence.

Why does this happen? Why do people have to sleep on the street?

There are lots of reasons why people are homeless. Owning or renting a home is expensive, and some people can't afford to do this. Some have an illness or disability that makes it difficult for them to work and make money, or to take care of themselves. Some homeless people are born into families who cannot take care of them. Others are born into families where they are hurt and neglected. They don't feel safe at home, so they choose not to live there. Sometimes people are homeless because they've lost their homes to a natural disaster like a fire or flood, or they are new to a community and are having difficulty finding a home.

Are there children who are homeless?

Yes. People of all ages can be homeless.

Young children who are homeless may live with their families in community shelters. These shelters provide families with food, warm clothing and basic services. Some families even live in their cars.

Older children are sometimes homeless because they have run away from their homes.

Why would someone run away from their home?

Some children live in homes where they are treated poorly or abused. They run away because they don't feel safe there. Children might also run away if they are neglected—if they do not feel important to their parents.

Sometimes parents cannot raise their children themselves and give them up. These children become *orphans*. They may end up in community homes or in temporary homes, called *foster* homes.

Children who run away and live on the street often feel like it is a better choice than living with their families or in homes where they do not feel loved or safe.

How can I help
children who are
homeless or unsafe?

There are many ways to help children in need. You and your family can donate resources to places in your community that help kids, like family shelters or Boys and Girls Clubs. You can also help raise awareness of children in need by choosing a charity that helps children and then organizing a fundraising activity at your local school, church, temple, mosque or synagogue.

If you think a child you know might need help, talk to an adult you trust—a parent, a teacher, a coach or a school counselor.

What Can I Do?

If you know someone who is neglected or abused, you can get them help in Canada by calling the Kids Help Phone (1-800-668-6868) or in the United States by calling the Childhelp National Child Abuse Hotline (1-800-4-A-Child, 1-800-422-4453).

UNICEF was established to help children in need all over the world. You can encourage your family to join the UNICEF monthly donor program. For more information, visit www.unicefusa.org or www.unicef.ca.

Look for a Boys and Girls Club in your community. These clubs offer programs and services for children of all ages.

Boys & Girls Clubs of Canada: www.bgccan.com

Boys & Girls Clubs of America: www.bgca.org

Was the man I saw sleeping on the street homeless as a child too?

He may have been, but he may not have been. He may have grown up in a loving and supportive family, but as an adult his situation changed. For example, he may have developed a physical or *mental illness*. When someone has an illness, it is very difficult to cope with daily life. Sometimes people are too sick to go to work, and then they cannot pay their bills or buy food. In these situations, people's health challenges lead to poverty and then to homelessness.

What Is Mental Illness?

It is any kind of disorder that results in people having abnormal thoughts, emotions and behaviors. These things affect their relationships with others.

Sometimes people are born with mental disorders, and sometimes they develop them as they get older. Mental illness can be caused by drug abuse, and people who have had a brain injury sometimes develop mental disorders.

Are homeless people the only ones who live in poverty?

No, being homeless is only one kind of poverty. There are other kinds of poverty that are harder to see, like when people are not able to go to school or to the doctor.

Don't all kids go to school?

No, not all kids are able to go to school, especially in developing countries in Africa, Asia and South America. Even in more prosperous countries, some kids do not receive a good education, and not all children have access to important classroom tools like computers and the Internet. Many are unable to go on to college, university or advanced job training. Without a good education, it can be very difficult to get a good job when you are older. When people do not receive a proper education, this is a sign of poverty.

"Education is recognized as a silver bullet around the world. Technology gives students an opportunity to take advantage of having all the world's information at your fingertips. We need to teach kids how to be strong digital leaders so they can take advantage of what they have in front of them."

—Jaime Casap, Education Evangelist, Google Inc.

A lack of education is a leading cause of poverty. Experts agree that equal access to quality education leads to a skilled workforce, and this is one of the most important ways to combat poverty.

—United Nations Educational, Scientific and Cultural Organization (UNESCO)

I go to my doctor whenever I get sick. Why doesn't everyone do that?

Not everyone is able to go see a doctor for regular checkups to make sure they stay healthy. When you are sick, you may need medicine that costs money, or you may need to travel to see a special doctor or take time off school or work for appointments. Not everyone can afford to do these things.

But being able to see a doctor when you are sick is an *essential service*. If children are not able to receive good health care, they may grow up with a physical or mental illness. When people do not receive proper health care, this is also a sign of poverty.

Families who are new to a community or a country often find it difficult to get the things they need. Without support from people in their community, they may not be able to do such things as find a doctor who is taking new patients. This is especially true for *refugees*.

What Are Essential Services?
These are things needed for a person to be healthy and safe. Without these things, lives are put at risk. Examples of essential services include access to food, water, medical care and protection.

What are refugees?

Refugees are people who have been forced to leave their homes and settle in a different country where the language, culture and customs are usually different from their own. This may happen because of a natural disaster or war. Refugees leave their homes because they do not feel safe, and everyone deserves to feel safe. Feeling safe is a fundamental human right.

On December 26, 2004, there was an earthquake in the Indian Ocean. It was the third largest ever recorded in human history. Devastating tsunamis followed that destroyed several coastal communities on the Indian Ocean. This terrible natural disaster killed many people and left thousands homeless.

In 2011, a civil war broke out in Syria. Since then, 13.5 million Syrians have required help from government agencies, and more than 6 million Syrians have fled their homes. Millions of Syrians have become refugees in neighboring countries and around the world. Much of the help for Syrian refugees has been provided by the United Nations High Commissioner for Refugees (UNHCR).

What Can I Do?

There are many refugee programs around the world. Many of these programs are supported by the UNHCR. You can help by researching refugee resettlement in your community and finding out how you can help make refugees feel welcome.

What is a fundamental human right?

Fundamental human rights are things that every human being deserves. Everyone deserves a home that they feel safe in. No one should have to go hungry. Everyone deserves to have access to schools and doctors.

The United Nations (UN) is an organization that was started to bring peace to all nations of the world. The UN wrote a special document that declared what rights everyone in the world should have. It is called the Universal Declaration of Human Rights. They also created a document that defines the rights of children specifically, called the UN Convention on the Rights of the Child.

"Every individual is equal before and under the law and has the right to the equal protection and equal benefit of the law without discrimination and, in particular, without discrimination based on race, national or ethnic origin, colour, religion, sex, age or mental or physical disability."
—Government of Canada, Canadian Charter of Rights and Freedoms

To see the UN Convention on the Rights of the Child In Child Friendly Language, visit www.unicef.org/rightsite/files/uncrcchilldfriendlylanguage.pdf

What can we do to help people who live in poverty?

One of the most important things you can do is care.

Ask questions. Remember that everyone matters, and we can work together to help those living in our community.

A lot of the work that needs to be done to end poverty is complicated, but you can talk to the adults in your life about it. You can talk about ways to celebrate people's differences, to help people feel proud of their backgrounds and abilities. And you can talk about ways schools and organizations in your community can support families who need help.

There are some things you and your family can do that will make an immediate difference. For example:

- Donate nonperishable food and toiletry items to food banks.

- Drop off new toys to fire halls during the holidays.

- Donate gently used clothing to charity.

- Introduce yourself to your neighbors (with your parents) or to children at your school who you don't know.

- Practice random acts of kindness to people living on the streets—a smile or a sandwich means a lot.

- Support refugee efforts in your community by volunteering your time.

- Celebrate diversity in your community by learning about a cultural celebration you don't know much about.

"Solutions to poverty go beyond handouts and 'giving money to poor people' in the form of government programs. Solving poverty is about providing opportunities. Often the difference between a kid living in poverty and one not living in poverty is opportunity. Opportunity for education. Opportunity for work."

—Jaime Casap, Education Evangelist, Google Inc.

When I first started to talk openly about growing up in poverty, it was difficult. People tend to correlate poverty with low ability and intelligence. But I did it because I wanted children who are growing up as I did to know that I am no different than they are and that they can accomplish anything. Reaching out to children to share these messages and break the assumptions about poverty is important to me. I couldn't have been more thrilled when Dr. Jillian Roberts contacted me to discuss her work and how we could educate children about issues of poverty so they could understand them and help solve the problems associated with it. As an expert in child psychology, Dr. Roberts was the perfect person to learn from and collaborate with. I am excited to work with her on this project and, hopefully, on many more to come. All children have tremendous capability and capacity if we give them the tools and opportunity. I hope this book inspires a thousand solutions to the problems of poverty and homelessness in the minds of the children who read these pages.

—Jaime Casap, Education Evangelist, Google Inc.

On one rainy afternoon, I came across a powerful quote that inspired me: "Don't ask kids what they want to be when they grow up; ask them what problem they want to solve." I have spent my life working with children, and I worry about the challenges they now face in our rapidly changing world. Our kids need to be prepared to face these challenges, and they will need to solve many problems along the way. It is essential that kids are educated to be effective problem solvers. With all this inspiration swirling around in my mind, I reached out to the brilliant person who wrote the quote that inspired me. His name is Jaime Casap, and he is Google's education evangelist. Jaime and I decided to work together on inspiring children to help solve one of the most pressing problems facing our world—homelessness. The result is this book. I hope it inspires you to help solve this problem!

—Dr. Jillian Roberts, child psychologist

Resources

Childhelp National Child Abuse Hotline (USA): www.childhelp.org/hotline/

Kids Help Phone (Canada): www.kidshelpphone.ca

UNESCO: en.unesco.org

UNICEF Canada: www.unicef.ca

UNICEF USA: www.unicefusa.org

United Nations Universal Declaration of Human Rights:
www.un.org/en/universal-declaration-human-rights/

UN Convention on the Rights of the Child In Child Friendly Language:
www.unicef.org/rightsite/files/uncrcchilldfriendlylanguage.pdf

World Health Organization: www.who.int